Road Trip Mini Journal

MATERIALS:

Road Trip Black paper • Road Trip stickers • 2 Red wire clips • Bottle caps: White and Red • Mini composition book • Photo • Red cardstock • Foam squares • Glue stick

INSTRUCTIONS:

Glue Road Trip Black paper to cover of book. Trim edges. • Mat photo with Red cardstock. Adhere to cover. • Flatten bottle caps and attach to cover with foam squares. Decorate caps with stickers. • Add Red clips.

Linen Mini Journal

MATERIALS:

Linen Houndstooth paper • Stickers: Black Words, Typewriter letter circles • Small White slide mount • Black metal clip • Mini composition book • Ivory ribbon • Photo • *ColorBox* Fluid Chalk Inkpads (Bisque, Amber Clay) • Foam squares • Tape • Glue stick

INSTRUCTIONS:

Glue Linen Houndstooth to cover of book. Trim edges. • Age edges with Amber Clay inkpad. Wrap book with Ivory ribbon, gluing in place and overlapping where photo will be positioned. • Cut small White mount in half, and age with Bisque inkpad. • Trim photo and tape to back of mount. • Attach to book with foam squares, hiding the ribbon overlap. • Add letter stickers to mount. Age edges of word stickers with Amber Clay inkpad and attach to book with foam squares.

School Days Mini Journal

MATERIALS:

Black Chalkboard paper • 2⅜" metal disk • Red metal clip • Black Words stickers • Mini composition book • Photo • Red acrylic paint • Cloth tape measure • Foam squares • Glue stick

INSTRUCTIONS:

Glue Black Chalkboard to cover of book. Trim edges. • Wrap book with tape measure, gluing in place and overlapping where photo will be positioned. • Paint metal disk with Red acrylic paint. Let dry. • Cut photo in circle to fit inside metal disk and glue in place. • Glue disk over tape measure. Attach word sticker to cover with foam squares. Add a Red metal clip.

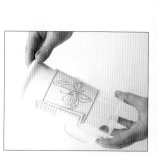

1. Unscrew mug and remove insert.

2. Trace insert onto back of paper.

3. Cut new insert from paper.

4. Arrange photos and stickers on front of new insert.

5. Slip decorated insert into mug and screw closed.

Terrific Tumblers

Make your morning drive a little merrier with these personalized coffee cups.

For Tall Tumbler

MATERIALS: Road Trip Black paper • Stickers: Text Messages, Black Words • Starbucks tumbler • Photos • Glue stick

For Medium Tumbler

MATERIALS: Road Trip Licenses paper • Stickers: Blue Words, Real Boy • Walgreen's tumbler • Photos • Glue stick

For Small Design a Mug

MATERIALS: Lime A-Z paper • Stickers: Blue Words, Flower Power • Design Mug • Photo • Glue stick

Pages 1-2: Cut square and rectangle from Linen Stripe. Sand edges and age with Charcoal ink. Glue square to left page, and rectangle to right page. • Attach Magic Mesh to right page, trimming as needed. • Position photos and glue in place. • Paint stencils and tags with gesso and let dry. Age with Creamy Brown ink. Glue stencils to left page. • Tie a bow in sheer ribbon, position on page and glue in place, wrapping ends around to back sides of page. • Stamp words on tags. Attach to right page with wire clips.

Pages 3-4: Cut square of Linen Houndstooth, and rectangles from Linen Houndstooth and Linen Large Floral. • Sand edges of Large Floral. • Dry brush top and bottom of Houndstooth pieces with Black acrylic, let dry. • Glue rectangles to left page, and square to right page. • Tear pieces of Ivory cardstock slightly larger than photos, age with Creamy Brown inkpad. Position aged cardstock and photos and glue in place. • Attach word stickers to left page with foam dots. • Cut small pieces of ribbon and staple to page. Attach word stickers and flattened bottle cap to right page with foam dots. • Thread fiber or twine through holes in tag stickers and tuck ends around Houndstooth paper. • Tie scraps of fibers in knot and trim as desired. Decorate bottle cap with sticker.

Pages 5-6: Cut squares of Linen Small Floral and Linen Vine, and rectangle of Linen Small Floral. Drybrush all pieces with gesso and let dry. • Crumple rectangle of Small Floral, flatten and age with Creamy Brown. Glue Small Floral square to left page, and Vines to right. • Add rectangle of Small Floral to right page as border. • Cut square of Black burlap. Fray edges and glue to left page. Position photo over burlap and glue in place. • Flatten bottle caps. Decorate caps and round tags with letter stickers. Attach bottle caps to page with foam dots, and metal tags with small brads. • Age small White envelope with Creamy Brown and Charcoal ink. Position photo and aged envelope on right page and glue in place. • Punch hole in metal disk and thread with fibers. Cut circle from scrap of Small Floral. Age with Charcoal ink and glue to disk. Glue disk in envelope.

Kraft Paper Album

This clever album is folded from one large piece of kraft paper. Use this same folding technique to make albums in any size or shape!

MATERIALS:
Papers: Linen Large Floral, Linen Large Stripe, Linen Houndstooth, Linen Small Floral, Linen Vine • 16" x 36" Brown craft paper • Ivory cardstock • 6 Silver bottle caps • Stickers: Typewriter ABCs, Art Elements, Black Words, Linen Tags • 2 Silver wire clips • Two 3" metal disks • 7 Black and White photos • Small White envelope • Assorted Black and White ribbons • Sheer Black ribbon • White twine or fibers • Black burlap • Black fibers or pearl cotton • White *Magic Mesh* • 2" letter stencils • 2 manila tags 1⅜" x 2¾" • 1¼" round metal-edge tags • 4 small Silver brads • Letter stamps • Black dye ink • *ColorBox* Chalk Inkpads (Charcoal, Creamy Brown) • Black acrylic • Gesso • Bristle brush • Sandpaper • Stapler • Hole punch • Foam tape • Foam dots • Glue stick

INSTRUCTIONS:
Scrapbook: Fold Brown paper according to the diagrams on page 5 to create scrapbook pages. • Punch holes ¾" from side fold and tie with ribbons, trimming to desired length. • If paper curls, hold in place with double-sided removable tape while working. For severe curling, place scrapbook on flat surface and weight with heavy books overnight.
Front cover: Cut square of Linen Large Floral. Sand edges. Glue to front cover, centering. • Tear a piece of Ivory cardstock slightly larger than photo. Age with Charcoal ink. Position aged cardstock and photo on cover. • Print "The many faces of" on Ivory cardstock. Cut out text in 2½" circle and age with Creamy Brown ink. Glue to metal disk. • Adhere to cover with foam tape. • Flatten bottle caps and attach to cover with foam dots. Decorate with letter stickers.

How To Fold
the Paper Album

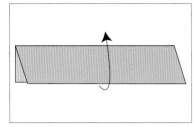

1. Fold paper in half lengthwise.

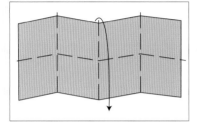

2. Open, fold in quarters widthwise and fold in half again lengthwise.

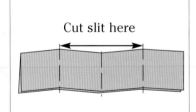

Cut slit here

3. Cut slit on horizontal fold line between outside folds.

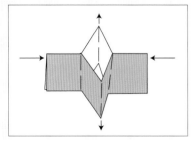

4. Fold in half horizontally from right to left, and fold in half again, with open edges to back.

5. Punch 6 holes down left side and tie with ribbons.

Emma
Door Hanger

MATERIALS:
Papers: Linen Diamond, Linen Small Floral • Stickers: Black Words, Linen Tags, Art Elements, Typewriter ABCs • Black bottle cap • Black cardstock • Chipboard (or 4" square coasters) • Muslin • Photo • Black brads • *ColorBox* Amber Clay Fluid Chalk inkpad • Gesso • Bristle brush • Hole punch • Foam squares • Glue stick

INSTRUCTIONS:
Cut two 4" squares of chipboard and round the corners.
• Punch 4 holes in one piece, and two holes in the second. Dry brush with gesso and let dry.
• Cut strips of Linen Diamond and Linen Small Floral papers. Glue Linen Diamond to chipboard with 4 holes, and Linen Floral to piece with 2 holes.
• Age both squares with Amber Clay inkpad.
• Tear strip of muslin and thread through holes at top of four hole piece to make handle, and through both pieces to attach.
• Flatten bottle cap and attach sticker.
• Put brads through tag stickers. Arrange all letters on top section, attaching with foam squares.
• Age Art Elements sticker with Amber Clay inkpad and attach to top section with foam squares.
• Mat photo with Black cardstock and attach to lower section with foam squares.
• Attach word stickers to lower section with foam squares.

Darling Door Hangers

These sweet and simple squares can be used as practical reminders to be quiet around baby's door, or to show off photos of the room's occupants.

Shh! Quiet Door Hanger

MATERIALS:
Papers: Baby Bubbles Blue, Baby Stripes • Brass bottle cap • 2⅜" metal disk • Stickers: Boy Sayings, Blue Words • Cardstock: Blue and White • Chipboard (or 4" square coasters) • Photo • Ivory sheer ribbon • Muslin • *ColorBox* Creamy Brown Fluid Chalk inkpad • Gesso • Bristle brush • Hole punch • E6000 adhesive • Foam squares • Glue stick

INSTRUCTIONS:
Cut two 4" squares of chipboard, and round the corners. • Punch 4 holes in one piece, and two holes in the second. Drybrush with gesso and let dry. • Cut strips of Baby Bubbles Blue and Baby Stripes. Glue stripes to chipboard with 4 holes, and bubbles to piece with 2 holes. • Age both squares with Creamy Brown inkpad. • Wrap ribbon vertically around 4-hole piece, and horizontally around 2-hole piece. • Tear strip of muslin, and thread through holes at top of 4-hole piece to make handle, and through both pieces to attach. • Print "Shh!" on White cardstock. Cut in circle and age with Creamy Brown. Glue to metal disk, and glue disk to top section of hanger. • Age word sticker and attach to top section with foam dots. • Mat photo with Blue cardstock and attach to bottom section with foam dots. • Flatten bottle cap and glue to bottom section. Decorate with sticker.

Creative Ideas for Metal Clips

Unleash your creativity with new ideas for using colorful metal clips and mini clothespins.

1. Attach a clip to the top of a Formica chip. Decorate with word stickers, and tie ribbon through the clip.
2. Clip cardstock decorated with word stickers to a piece of torn fabric.
3. Use mini clothespins to hold letter tags.
4. Flatten bottle caps and decorate with letter stickers. Add clip to top, and attach to page with brad through back hole in clip.
5. Use clip to attach decorated tag to envelope. Tie a piece of ribbon to clip.
6. Use mini clothespins to attach metal-edge tags and streamers to ribbon.
7. Clip several small pieces of paper together to make a mini book.
8. Mount a small photo in a slide mount. Decorate with word stickers and use binder clips to attach it to a layout.
9. Use a mini clothespin to hold the center of a ribbon bow, and a vellum tag decorated with a word sticker.
10. Clip mini file folders to a layout.
11. Attach either tulle or ribbon to a page. Gather and clip with a mini clothespin. Tuck in a tag decorated with a bottle cap sticker.
12. Use mini clothespins to clip a small piece of fabric, letter stickers, or other embellishments to a hemp cord clothesline.

Canvas

MATERIALS:
- 12" x 12" art canvas
- Papers: Dictionary, Watermarks, Vintage ABCs
- 3 Black bottle caps • Art Elements stickers
- 1¾" x 7¾" pencil box
- 4 Mini brads
- Black *Magic Mesh*
- 2 Black photo mounting corners
- 4 Daisy metal eyelets • Metal alphabet brads
- Letter eyelets
- Key charm
- *DMC floss:* Black, Gray, Silver)
- 3 Silver rivets
- 'moment' label
- Hat pin
- Glass pebble
- Butterfly sticker
- *ColorBox* Cat's Eye Chestnut Roan ink
- *Tsukineko* StazOn Jet Black ink
- Rubber Stamps (*Hero Arts*: Manuscript background, Italian Poetry; *Limited Edition* Doll body stamp; *Stampcraft* Ransom Numbers; *Stampmania* Imagine)
- Sanding block
- Paintbrush
- Craft knife
- Eyelet tools
- Fiskars ¹⁄₁₆" hand punch
- Needle
- *Therm O Web* (Zots, Memory Tape Runner, Zots 3D)
- Packing Tape
- E6000 adhesive

Creative Canvas with Nicho

by Diana McMillan

Add an extra layer of dimension to your canvas with this neat technique. Use a pencil case to add a shadowbox to your canvas.

INSTRUCTIONS:
Paint the canvas Red. Let dry. Sand to distress. • Stamp "Imagine", "Italian Poetry", and "that it will never come again" with Black. • Adhere Magic Mesh. • Sand and rub paint on eyelet letters. • Set eyelets, 3 Silver rivets, and brad letters. • Trace around the pencil box on the canvas. Cut away the canvas on the lines. • Remove the lid from the pencil box. Line the inside of the pencil box with Dictionary paper and let the paper extend past the edges. Cut Vintage ABC paper into diamond shape. Ink the edges with Chestnut Roan. Adhere the diamonds inside the pencil box. • Position and tape the pencil box to the back of the canvas. • Rub Sunflower paint on the photo corners. Place photo in corners and adhere to canvas. • Stamp the doll body on Watermark paper. Stamp the arms and legs with Manuscript background. Adhere the doll parts to chipboard. Cut out the doll. Attach the arms and legs to the body with mini brads. • Sand daisies. Rub daisies with Sunflower and Poppy. • Flatten bottle caps. Hammer the edges to form a square. Punch a hole in the middle of the cap with the Fiskars punch. Attach 2 daisies to bottle caps with Cream brads. Layer 2 more daisies together and attach to the canvas with a Black brad. • Attach Black floss to the key charm and adhere to the canvas with E6000. • Make a tassel with floss or purchase one. Punch a hole in the top of the pencil box with a needle and thread the tassel through the hole. Tie a knot to secure.

Journal and Jar

Stop writer's block with these journaling prompts. Next time you want to write but can't seem to get started, just reach into the jar and pull out a fresh writing assignment.

MATERIALS
Composition book • Papers: Linen Houndstooth, Linen Diamond • Two 3" metal disks • Glass jar • Taupe cardstock • Black burlap • Black ultrasuede • Ivory voile • Photos or photocopies • Rub-on alphabet • Small tags • Word stamps • Label holder • *ColorBox* Amber Clay Fluid Chalk Inkpad • Black dye ink • Pen • Hole punch • E6000 adhesive • Double-stick tape • Glue stick

INSTRUCTIONS:
Journal: Cover front and back sections of composition book with Linen Houndstooth paper.
• Cut 4" wide strip of ultrasuede. Coat one side of ultrasuede with glue stick and wrap around book spine. Let dry completely. • Cut small square of burlap and fray edges by pulling threads. Glue to front of book. • Cut photo in 2½" circle and glue into metal disk. Glue to front of book with E6000.
• Attach label holder to book following manufacturer's instructions.
• Apply rub-on to small scrap of cardstock and insert in label holder. • Tear a strip of voile and fray edges by pulling threads. Tie around front cover. Age cover and fabric with Amber Clay inkpad. • Age tag with Amber Clay. Stamp word with Black dye ink and tie to journal.
Jar: Cut strip of Linen Diamond paper. Age edges with Amber Clay inkpad. Wrap around glass jar, holding with double-stick tape until positioned properly. • Apply glue stick to hold in place. • Cut small square of Black burlap and fray edges by pulling threads. Glue to paper around jar. • Apply rub-on to metal disk. • Punch hole in disk at top. Tear two strips of voile and fray edges by pulling threads. Tie one strip through metal disk and around neck of jar.
• Tie other strip around paper, trimming ends as desired. Age fabric with Amber Clay inkpad. • Age tags with Amber Clay and stamp words with Black dye ink. Tie tags to fabric strip holding metal disk.
• Tuck photo into fabric strip and hold in place with double-sided tape.
• Print journal prompts on Taupe cardstock and cut into individual pieces. Fold and place in jar.

Journal Prompts

Here's a list of prompts to get you started filling your own journal jar. Anything you'd like someone in your family to write about can be added.

Write about...
something for which you are grateful
what you like to read
your favorite book and why it's your favorite
your favorite types of movies
your all-time favorites movies
your favorite or least favorite job
the best year you ever had
your favorite teacher
your favorite school memories
something that drives you crazy
a talent you have and how you developed it
your grandparents
your father
your mother
your brothers
your sisters
your best family memories
your favorite part of growing up
your hardest good-bye
the first time you lived away from home
your best Thanksgiving or Christmas
your favorite vacation
a favorite family pet
your first driving experience
your worst cooking disaster
the birth of your 1st child
the cutest thing one of your children ever did
your feelings on being a parent
your best birthday and best birthday gift
your first love
your most embarrassing moment
the kindest things anyone ever did for you
the funniest things that ever happened to you
the place you chose to marry and why
who was at your wedding
what you remember about your wedding day
the first time you told each other, "I love you"
what you most daydream about
your favorite food and why it's your favorite
what you are afraid of and why
the first place you ever remember living
something or someone you remember fondly
the best party you ever went to
when your first child left home
the loss of someone close to you
your best friend
your child's first day of school
buying your first home

Teacher's Pet File Folder

MATERIALS:
Papers: Black Chalkboard, Vintage ABCs • Stickers: Road Trip ABC Tags • 3" metal disk • 2 Manila mini file folders • Manila office file folder • Cardstock: Manila, Black • 7 small Silver brads • Tape measure • Big Yellow pencil • Chalk • Label maker • Black label tape • Letter stamps • *ColorBox* Yellow Ochre Fluid Chalk inkpad • Black pigment ink • Black embossing powder • Spray sealer • E6000 adhesive • Foam squares • Glue stick

INSTRUCTIONS:
Outside: Write "Teacher's Pet" on Black cardstock. Spray with sealer. Trim to size. Glue to front of folder.
• Age folder with chalk inkpad. • Wrap front page of folder with tape measure, overlapping and gluing in place inside folder.
Inside of Folder: Cover the left side of folder with Black Chalkboard paper. Cut a strip of Vintage ABCs 8" x 11½". Tear edge and age with chalk ink. Glue to right side of folder. • Age folder with chalk inkpad.
• Mat photo with manila cardstock. Age edges of mat and attach photo to folder with foam squares.
• Age small folders with chalk inkpad. Stamp with Black pigment ink. Glue folders in place with foam squares. To give folders dimension, tuck a foam square inside each one before closing. • Stamp metal disk with text. Emboss with Black embossing powder. Glue to folder with E6000.
• Put brads through holes in tag stickers and attach to folder with foam squares. • Write name with labelmaker on Black label tape and attach to folder. • Cut squares from Vintage ABCs and age with chalk inkpad. Attach to front of folder with foam squares.
• Glue pencil to front of folder with E6000.

Field Trip Clipboard

MATERIALS:
Road Trip Black paper • Stickers: Road Trip ABC Tags, Road Trip • 3 Black bottle caps • 2⅜" metal disk • 6" x 9" clipboard • Photo • Plexiglass • Yellow cardstock • Magnet • Small Black brads • Assorted ribbons • *Making Memories* Simply Stated rub-ons • Black acrylic paint • Taupe spray paint • E6000 adhesive • Foam squares • Glue stick

INSTRUCTIONS:
Spray paint clipboard with Taupe. Let dry.
• Cut Road Trip Black paper slightly smaller than clipboard and glue in place.
• Apply rub-ons to clamp and plexiglass.
• Slide photo and plexiglass under clamp.
• Paint metal disk with Black acrylic. Let dry.
• Print "Field" on Yellow cardstock and cut out to fit inside the metal disk. Adhere circle to painted disk. • Attach disk to clipboard with E6000 and bottle caps with foam squares. • Apply stickers to bottle caps.
• Put brads through holes in tag stickers and adhere to clipboard with foam squares.
• Clip small pieces of ribbons and tie to clamp.

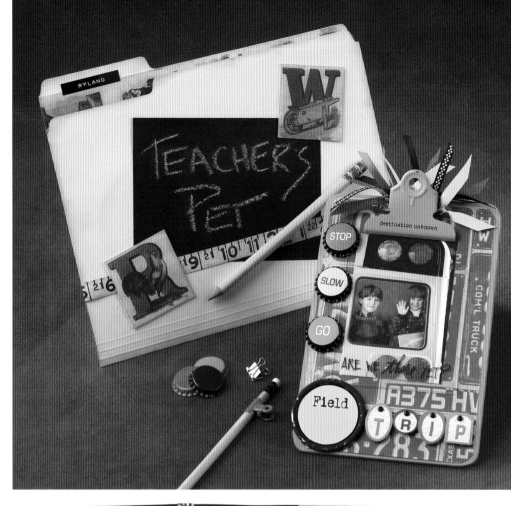

File Folder and Clipboard

Why hide all those fun field trip memories in an album? Display them on a clipboard. If you have too many, arrange the photos on a wall or bulletin board and use this clipboard as your title section.

Display your school days layout in a portable folder. Leave it on the coffee table for folks to peruse.

Page 1: Inside front cover: Print text on Blue cardstock. Tear out and age with Prussian Blue inkpad. Wrap ribbon from front cover around, overlap, and clamp with Blue wire clips. Glue ribbon and text in place if desired.

Page 2: We Love You Dad: Tear Mosaic Blue paper 7½" x 9" and age with Prussian Blue inkpad. Glue to first divider. Age divider with Prussian Blue. • Mat photo with Navy cardstock. Cut three 4" lengths of Blue ribbon, fold in half, and staple to photo. • Attach cardstock to page with foam tape. • Cut circle from Mosaic Circles paper and glue to 3" metal disk. Flatten bottle cap and glue to disk with E6000. • Write words with labelmaker and Blue label tape. Decorate cap with sticker. Adhere cap to disk with E6000.

For Dad Album

Rethink your definition of what books are and are made of with this very masculine looking reinterpretation of a classification folder. Dad is going to love this one, with its rich colors, intriguing textures and sweet sentiments. The folders give you plenty of space on which to express your creativity and love for Dad.

MATERIALS:
Papers: Mosaic Blue, Mosaic Circles, Mosaic Rust, Mosaic Tiles, Vellum Shorthand • Stickers: Mosaic ABC Tags, Blue ABCs, Walnut ABCs, Art Words • Metal disks: One 2⅜", two 3" • Wire clips: 2 Blue, 1 Silver • 9 Silver bottle caps • 10" x 12" Pressboard letter-size classification folder with 2 dividers • Cardstock: Rust, Navy, Blue, Ochre, Hunter • Manila tags (2 small, 1 large) • Ribbon: 22" Ochre, 12" Blue • Hemp cord • 7 small Silver brads • 2" stencils • Labelmaker • Label tape: Blue, Green • ColorBox Fluid Chalk inkpads: Chestnut Roan, Prussian Blue, Raw Sienna, Moss Green • Brown dye ink • Letter stamps • Craft knife • Ruler • Dremel drill • ⅛" drill bit • E6000 adhesive • Foam tape • Foam squares • Glue stick

INSTRUCTIONS:
Creating album: See photos on page 11. • Draw a line 8" from bottom of classification folder. Cut folder on line using sharp craft knife and a ruler. Round corners of folder and dividers.
Cover: Age edges of front cover with Chestnut Roan inkpad. Cut Mosaic Tiles paper 7" x 8½" and glue to front cover. Glue Ochre ribbon to front cover, leaving tails long enough to wrap to inside and overlap. • Trace DAD on Rust cardstock using 2" stencils. Cut out letters using craft knife. Age with Chestnut Roan inkpad. Cut small piece of Vellum Shorthand and tape to back of stencil. Mount to front cover using foam tape. • Attach tag letters to front cover using foam squares. Thread ribbon through holes and tie in knots, trimming as desired. • Write text with labelmaker and orange label tape and attach to tab.

Pages 3 & 4: Without You: Tear 2 pieces of Mosaic Rust paper 7½" x 9". Age with Raw Sienna. Glue to pages. • Age edges of pages with Raw Sienna. Mat photos with Ochre cardstock and attach to pages with foam tape. • Cut circle from Ochre cardstock. Age tags and circle with Chestnut Roan inkpad. Glue circle to center of small metal disk. Stamp words on tags and disk with Brown dye ink. Flatten 4 bottle caps. Arrange tags, bottle caps and disk on left page. Adhere metal pieces with E6000 and tags with glue stick. Attach large tag to left side of layout with wire clip.

Pages 5 & 6: Come Home Soon: Tear Mosaic Circles paper 7" x 8½". Age with Moss Green inkpad. Glue to pages. Age left page with Moss Green ink. • Mat photo with Green cardstock. • Drill hole in 3" metal disk. Cut circle and glue to disk. Write text with labelmaker and Green label tape. Attach to disk. Thread hemp cord through hole in disk and knot, leaving long tails. Attach disk to page with foam tape. • Adhere photo to page with foam tape, wrapping tail underneath. Tie knot in top of cords, around photo, and trim. • Insert brads through holes in tag stickers. • Flatten bottle caps and decorate with stickers. Cut strip of 4 Mosaic Tiles and decorate with letter stickers. • Position elements on page and adhere with foam squares and E6000.

Cutting Down a Folder

1. Draw a line 8" from the bottom.

2. Cut through all layers with craft knife.

3. Round corners using cut piece as a guide.

4. Edge with chalk inks.

Clipboard Frame

Hang a clipboard in your game room or office and show off your family. As the seasons change, alternate photos of basketball, baseball and football to keep the wall display interesting all year long.

by Michele Charles

MATERIALS:

6" x 9" clipboard • Papers: Sports Pennants, Sports Letters • 3 Red bottle caps • Red ABCs stickers • Two 3" photos • Ribbons • *Delta Ceramcoat* Orange acrylic paint • *ColorBox* Sepia Black pigment ink • Two 3" squares Plexiglass • Vaseline • Paintbrush • Adhesive Foam Squares • Glue

INSTRUCTIONS:

Paint clipboard Orange. Let dry. • Sponge paint onto metal clip. Let dry. • Apply a second coat. Let dry. • Tear Sports Pennants paper 5¼" x 7¾". Edge with Sepia Black ink. Glue to clipboard. • Edge painted clipboard with Sepia Black ink. • Cut out letter T from Sports Letters paper. Attach with foam squares. • Flatten 3 Red bottle caps and attach to clipboard with foam squares. Apply stickers to caps. Attach to clipboard with foam squares. • Rub a thin layer of Vaseline onto Plexiglass only where the main image of photo will appear. Apply Orange paint to Plexiglass going over the Vaseline. Let dry. • Gently wipe Vaseline off of Plexiglass. Place photo beneath Plexiglass. If needed, softly scratch off paint with fingernail or cloth to reveal more of the photo image. Adhere Plexiglass to clipboard. • Tie ribbons to back of metal clip.

Round Metal Disks

Metal disks are so-o-o decorative! Whether you use them as a stand-alone project or as an embellishment, you are going to appreciate the versatility of this accent.

1. Paint metal disk with *Ranger* Adirondack acrylics. Cut circle from photo and glue to painted lid. Apply word sticker and sequin star with foam dots.

2. Cut circle from patterned paper and glue to metal disk. Flatten bottle cap and adhere to lid with foam square. Decorate cap with bottle cap sticker and clear epoxy sticker.

3. Cut circle from photo and glue to metal disk. Attach lid to project with matching metal clip.

4. Age small envelope with chalk inks and stamp as desired. Drill hole in metal disk and thread with paper raffia or fibers. Apply rub-on to metal disk.

5. Cut circle from patterned paper and apply word sticker. Pile star sequins in center of circle and glue top of button to paper. Let set until completely dry. Glue to metal disk.

6. Paint metal disk with gesso. While still wet, cut circle from transparency sheet and place in center of lid. Let dry. Dab with glitter glue to add sparkle.

7. Cut a circle from photo. Glue to metal disk. Dab edges of circle with glue and apply microbeads.

8. Drill holes through five metal disks. Paint with metallic acrylics. Let dry. Thread split ring through holes. Cut circles from photos and glue to lids. Decorate with word stickers.

9. Cut circle from patterned paper and edge with chalk inks. Glue to metal disk. Remove silk flower from stem and glue to lid. Use labelmaker to add text.

10. Cut photo and apply to metal disk. Drill holes in bottom of lid and hang letter charms with jump rings. Apply metal letters to photo.

11. Cut circle from paper. Edge with chalk inkpad. Glue silk ribbon across circle. Glue to metal disk. Tie bow from silk ribbon and glue to lid. Age letter with chalk inkpad. Apply letter with foam dots.

12. Cut circle from paper and edge with chalk inks. Glue to metal disk. Cut heart from patterned paper and age with chalk ink. Glue strip of silk ribbon across heart. Decorate with metal letters and small buttons. Attach to metal disk with foam dots.

This charming photo is perfect for framing. Multiple layers and great use of color draw your eye into this attractive art.

MATERIALS
Papers: Mosaic Blue, Mosaic Rust, Mosaic Tiles • Blue metal clips • Black bottle cap • Art Elements stickers • 12" x 12" art canvas • Cardstock • 1" tagboard letter stencils • Natural burlap • Silk sunflower • Yellow Ochre acrylic paint • *ColorBox* Chestnut Roan Fluid Chalk inkpad • *Ranger* TeaDye Distress Inkpad • Twill tape • E6000 adhesive • Foam tape • Glue stick

INSTRUCTIONS:
Paint canvas with acrylic paint. Let dry. Age edges of canvas with Chestnut Roan inkpad. • Mat photo with Mosaic Rust paper and back with cardstock to support. • Print text on twill tape. Wrap twill tape around bottom of photo and glue in place.
• Cut a strip of Mosaic Tiles 2 blocks high for the bottom border, and a piece of Mosaic Blue 8½" wide. Glue to canvas and let dry completely.
• TeaDye letter stencils with Distress ink. Add Blue clip to the top of each letter. Position clipped letters on canvas, holding in place with E6000 on clip and foam tape on stencil.
• Cut a piece of burlap 7" x 10" and pull threads to fray edges. Glue to canvas at an angle. Glue photo over burlap. • Remove center from sunflower and glue layers of petals together. Glue flower to canvas. Glue bottle cap to center of flower. Decorate cap with sticker.

Tag in the Pocket:

Print journaling on an 8½" x 11" sheet of cardstock. Trim the top and bottom right hand corners to create a tag shape. Ink the edges.
• Mat photo with Ochre. Adhere to tag.
• Punch a hole in the middle of the right edge. Thread string through the hole.

Friends Catching Up page: Cut da Vinci Brocade just smaller than height of bag. Age edges with sandpaper. Glue to bag, overlapping center fold and continuing under flap. • Turn page to create center crease. Sand crease. • Mat photo on Ochre cardstock and glue to top of page. • Paint stencils with Ochre acrylic. When dry, age with Raw Sienna inkpad. • Put brads through holes in tag stickers. Position stickers and stencils on page and attach with foam squares.

Paper Bag Album

Rewrite your definition of "album" with this extraordinary handmade paper bag book. Paper bag books provide the artist with an exceptional amount of canvas on which to display their art in the form of flaps, pages and pockets.

Cover: Tear Dictionary paper just smaller than cover. • Crumple paper tightly, then uncrumple. Age center with Bisque inkpad, and outer edges with Amber Clay. Let dry. Smooth paper completely by dragging across edge of table, holding tautly. Glue to front of album. • Cut a strip 2 squares wide from da Vinci Tiles paper. Glue to left side of cover. • Print "Friends" on Ochre cardstock. Age with Raw Sienna inkpad. Tape to large mount.
• Punch holes in corners of mount and insert brads in holes. • Age small tag with Bisque inkpad. • Attach stickers to small tag. Put large brad through hole.
• Insert small brads in the holes of tag stickers. • Position all elements on front cover and attach with foam dots.

Friends page: Cut Legacy Gold Stripe slightly smaller than bag flap. Age edges with sandpaper. Glue to flap. • Fold right side of flap back to create crease. Sand across crease. • Flatten 7 bottle caps and attach to right side of flap with foam dots. • Attach stickers to caps. • Print text on large manila tags. Age with Bisque inkpad. Trim photos to roughly 2" square and glue to tags. • Age string with Chestnut Roan inkpad. Thread through tags. • Glue tags in place beneath flap as shown.

Bulletin Board Clipboard

Post all those notes about prom, graduation rehearsal, and final exams on a small cork square right under Your favorite photo. This is a great gift for graduating seniors.

MATERIALS:
Papers: TeaDye Script, da Vinci Brocade, da Vinci Tiles • Stickers: Walnut Numbers, da Vinci Tags • 4 Brass bottle caps • Clipboard • Photo • Plexiglass • 12" of 2" wide Ivory organza ribbon • Small brass brad • 3½" x 4½" piece of cork • Pushpins • Rub-ons alphabet • *ColorBox* Chalk inkpads (Amber Clay, Chestnut Roan) • Brown spray paint • Gold acrylic paint • Bristle brush • Foam squares • E6000 adhesive • Glue stick

INSTRUCTIONS:
Basecoat clipboard with Brown spray paint. Let dry completely. • Drybrush clamp with Gold acrylic. Let dry. • Cover clipboard with TeaDye Script paper, adhering with glue stick. Trim around edges when dry.
• Tear da Vinci Brocade. Ink the torn edge with Amber Clay. Glue to lower section of clipboard.
• Cut a 2 block vertical strip of da Vinci Tiles. Glue to side of clipboard, lining up right side and bottom edges. Let papers dry. • Age all edges with Chestnut Roan and Amber Clay. •Glue the cork square to lower left section of clipboard with E6000. • Apply rub-on to Plexiglass. Slide photo and Plexiglass under clamp, centering. • Flatten bottle caps and apply to page with foam squares. Decorate with stickers.
• Put brad through holes of letter tag stickers, and apply to page.
• Fray edges of organza ribbon. Tie in a knot around the clamp.

Printing Tags on the Computer

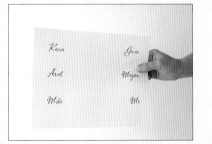

1. Print test on plain paper.

2. Line up tags over text and tape with double-sided tape.

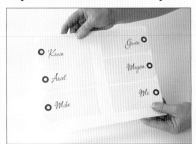

3. Print using heavy card-stock setting.

MATERIALS:
Papers: da Vinci Brocade, da Vinci Tiles, Dictionary, Legacy Gold Stripe • 3½" square Tapes slide mount • 7 Brass bottle caps • Stickers: Walnut ABCs, da Vinci Tag • 3 large paper bags • Cardstock (Ochre, Ivory) • Photos • Gold brads (16 small, 1 large) • Manila Tags (One 1½" x 2¾", Six 2⅜" x 4¾") • String • 2" stencils • *ColorBox* Fluid Chalk inkpads (Amber Clay, Bisque, Raw Sienna, Chestnut Roan) • Ochre acrylic paint • Sewing machine • Hole punch • Sandpaper • Tape • Foam dots • Glue stick

INSTRUCTIONS:
For album: Stack 3 paper bags on top of each other, alternating openings right, left, right. Fold in half. Stitch bags on fold.

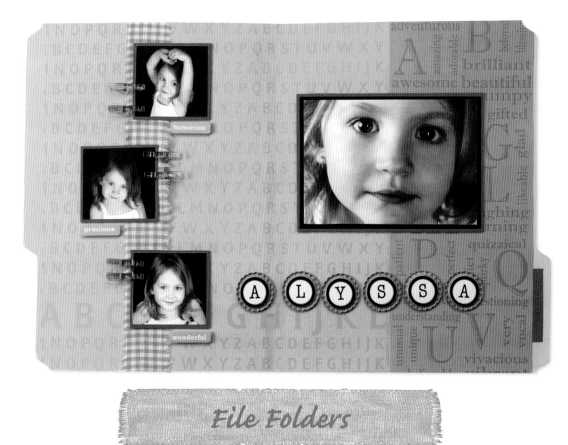

File Folders

Capture a moment in time with a set of photos. For the novice scrapper, this is a wonderful way to develop scrapbooking skills without having to fill an entire book. A folder makes the perfect display for your best baby and child photos. This is a nice gift for Grandma to place on her table to show all her friends.

You can also keep memorabilia that is too bulky to put in a scrapbook, such as the daily paper from the date of birth.

'Girl' File Folder

MATERIALS:
Papers: Pink A-Z Word Blocks, Pink A-Z • 6 Pink clothespins • 3" metal disk • 6 Pink bottle caps • Stickers: Typewriter ABCs, Pink Words • Cardstock: Pink, Purple, Black • Pink file folder • Purple gingham • Pink paint sample card • Letter stencils • Labelmaker • Markers • E6000 adhesive • Foam squares • Glue stick

INSTRUCTIONS:
Interior: Glue a full sheet of Pink A-Z paper to inside of folder. • Cut a 5" wide strip of Pink A-Z Word Blocks and glue to right side of folder.
• Tear a 1¾" wide strip of gingham and tie around folder, leaving long tails on exterior of folder.
• Mat small photos with Purple cardstock. Attach foam squares to back, and space evenly along strip of gingham, alternating placement. Attach clips to edges of photos. Position stickers below each photo. Adhere with foam squares.
• Mat large photo with Black cardstock, then again with Purple cardstock. Attach to folder with foam squares.
• Flatten bottle caps and attach to page with E6000. Decorate with Typewriter ABC stickers.
• Cut strip of Purple cardstock and feed into labelmaker. Write name with labelmaker and trim to size. If desired, brush embossed letters with marker or inkpad to make letters stand out.
Exterior: Untie knot in gingham. Cut piece of A-Z Word Blocks and glue to left side of folder. Glue paint sample card over paper at an angle. Tie gingham in a knot, trimming tails as desired and fraying edges.
• Glue metal disk to folder with E6000. Cut circle from Pink cardstock. Stencil initial on circle and glue to center of disk.

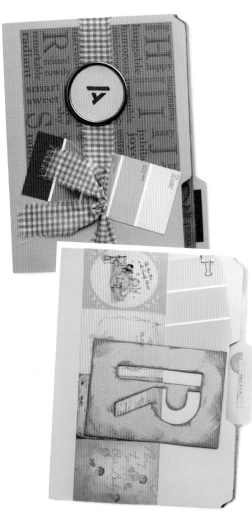

'Boy' File Folder

MATERIALS:
Papers: Baby Books, Baby Stripes, Baby Bubbles Blue • Blue Tag ABCs stickers • White wire clips • Blue file folder • Cardstock: Pink, White • Star shaped brads • Yellow paint sample card • Newspaper • Envelope • Letter stencils • *ColorBox* Rouge Fluid Chalk inkpad • Labelmaker • Craft knife • Foam squares • Glue stick

INSTRUCTIONS:
Interior: Cut around ribbon of Baby Stripes paper, leaving 1¾" attached at either side. Glue to left side of folder, leaving cut section unglued. • Tear left edge of Baby Bubbles paper, age with inkpad and glue to left side of folder, crossing over fold and covering edge of stripes. • Fold White cardstock to create pocket, and glue to bottom of left side.
• Cut Baby Books paper into 3 strips. Glue 1 strip over cardstock pocket, across fold in folder. Glue second piece to left side of folder, trimming as necessary. • Mat photos with Pink cardstock, leaving a 1⅜" border at bottom of one photo.
• Write name with tag stickers in border, sliding star brads through holes. Attach to right side of folder. • Tuck photo, newspaper and envelope into pocket, sliding photo under cut section of paper.
• Cut a strip of Pink cardstock and write name with labelmaker. Trim and glue to folder. If desired, brush embossed letters with marker or inkpad to make letters stand out.
Exterior: Glue remaining strip of Baby Books paper to folder, leaving a section with no glue so you can slide paint sample card under paper, and hold in place with White wire clip.
• Stencil letter on Pink cardstock, and cut out. Age with chalk ink and attach to folder with a wire clip.

Clipboard Frame

by Michele Charles

When you want something more interesting than the usual photo frame, try this clipboard. The "vaseline resist" technique allows you to paint on Plexiglass.

MATERIALS:
Papers: Pink A-Z, Lime A-Z • 3 Aqua bottle caps • 3 Pink clothespins • Stickers: Pink Words, Princess • 6" x 9" clipboard • 4" x 6" photo • 4" x 6" plexiglass • *Delta Ceramcoat* acrylic paint: Lisa Pink, Turquoise, Colonial Blue • *ColorBox* Chalk Rouge ink • Vaseline • Paintbrush • Foam Squares • Glue

INSTRUCTIONS:
Paint clipboard and sponge the metal clip with Colonial Blue. Let dry. Apply a second coat. Let dry. • Tear Lime A-Z paper 5¼" x 7¾". Glue to clipboard. Dry brush clipboard with Turquoise and Lisa Pink paints. • Tear Pink A-Z paper 4¼" x 5¾". Edge with Rouge ink. Glue over Lime paper on clipboard. • Flatten 3 Aqua bottle caps and adhere to clipboard with foam squares. Add Princess stickers to caps. • Rub a thin layer of Vaseline onto Plexiglass only where the main image of photo will appear. Apply Turquoise paint to Plexiglass, going over the Vaseline. Let dry. Gently wipe Vaseline off of Plexiglass. Place photo beneath Plexiglass. If needed, softly scratch off paint with fingernail or cloth to reveal more of the photo image. • Attach 3 Pink word stickers to Lime A-Z paper. Trim 2 words strips with ½" tab on left and ⅛" border on all other sides. Trim 1 word strip with ½" tab on right and ⅛" border on all other sides. Adhere to clipboard with foam squares and then attach Pink clothespins. • Tie ribbons to back of metal clip.

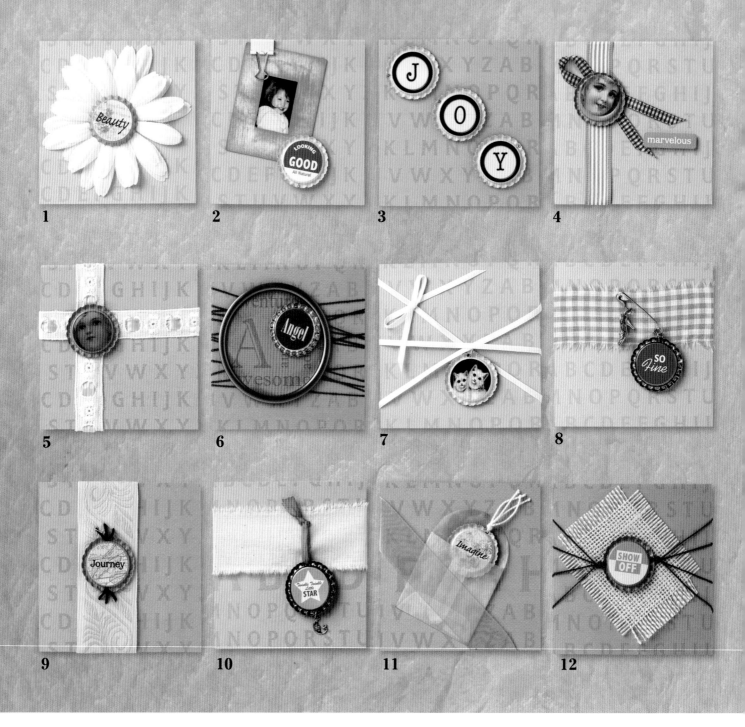

Bottle Cap Accents

I make my own accents so my pages are unique and interesting. This also coordinates the color and style with the theme of my page. I hope these ideas will inspire you to make your own exciting embellishments.

1. Remove stem and center from silk daisy. Glue to page and fill center with bottle cap.
2. Attach a bottle cap to the corner of a slide mount to accent a framed photo.
3. Use bottle caps and stickers to spell out words for titles.
4. Flatten bottle cap and apply a sticker. Glue over ribbon loops, bow or a torn piece of fabric.
5. Apply a vintage image to a flattened bottle cap, and cover with a clear epoxy sticker. Apply over pieces of lace or ribbon.
6. Cut a paper circle, edge with ink, and glue to a metal disk. Apply sticker to flattened bottle cap and glue inside rim of metal disk.
7. Flatten bottle cap, punch a hole in the rim with a 1/16" hole punch or nail, and hang from a jump ring. Rings can be threaded onto ribbon,

pearl cotton, fibers or through loosely woven fabrics or twill tape.
8. Punch a hole in the cap rim and use a safety pin to attach to fabric or ribbon. Hang a charm from the pin before closing.
9. Punch holes in opposite sides of bottle cap rim, and stitch to ribbon or fabric with pearl cotton or floss.
10. Punch holes in opposite sides of rim. Hang cap from pearl cotton, floss or ribbons stitched through fabric. Hang a charm from bottom of cap.
11. Use bottle caps as tags! Just punch a hole in the rim and thread a few strands of fibers or rayon floss through. These look great slipped into clear or vellum envelopes.
12. Punch holes on opposite sides of the cap rim, and thread onto ribbon, floss or fibers.

by Michele Charles

Whether it's a boy or girl, or twins, these matching canvases allow you to make a joyful display to celebrate the arrival of your little one.

Mini Canvas Collage

MATERIALS:
Baby Stripes paper • Stickers: Pink Tag ABCs, Blue Tag ABCs, Blue Words • Large White slide mount • Wire clips: White, Pink • 6" x 6" art canvas • Ribbon • Photo • *Delta* Ceramcoat Paints: Lisa Pink, Colonial Blue, Light Ivory • Paintbrush • Craft knife • Foam dots • Tape • Glue

INSTRUCTIONS:
Paint canvas and slide mount Pink or Blue. Let dry. • Cut a 6" x 6" square from the upper right corner of the Baby Stripe paper. Tear in half diag-onally. Use the portion with bow and flowers. • Do a Lift Technique on the Baby Stripes paper by cutting around bow loops and flowers with a craft knife. Glue paper to canvas but do not glue down bow and flowers.
• Dry brush lightly on canvas and slide mount with Light Ivory and either Pink or Blue paints. • Cut out photo and tape to back of slide mount. • Tie rib-bons to wire clip. Attach clip to bottom left corner of slide mount. Place Blue Words stickers on slide mount. Place the mount under lift area and press to canvas. • Tie ribbon to each tag sticker and adhere to canvas with foam dots.

Paper Bag Album

Choose your favorite word stickers to describe this page. Squeeze in a personal handwritten message too.

This project is so neat... it is perfect for friends to make at a pajama party.

MATERIALS:
Papers: Pink A-Z Word Blocks, Pink A-Z • 3½" square Diamonds slide mount • 3 White wire clips • Bottle caps: 3 Pink, 1 Silver • Metal disks: One 2⅜", one 3" • Stickers: Citrus circles, Princess circles, Pink Words • 3 small Pink paper bags • Cardstock: Pink, Lavender, Fuchsia, Purple • 6 photos • Large manila tag • Paint sample cards • Metal letters • Acrylic button top • Large and small star-shaped brads • Ribbons: 1 yard Pink, Magenta • White tulle • Silver metallic floss • Star sequins • Small and large letter stamps • *ColorBox* Fluid Chalk inkpads: Wisteria, Peony, Warm Violet • Iridescent glitter glue • Punches: Large daisy, ¼" circle • Stapler • Drill • Craft knife • E6000 adhesive • Foam squares • Foam tape • Tape

INSTRUCTIONS:
Album Assembly: Stack 3 Pink bags as follows: flap on left side, flap on right side, flap on left side. Fold bags in half. Punch holes on fold at top and bottom. • It is easier to work with these bags if you tie them together after you decorate them. You may wish to number the pages lightly with a pencil.

Cover: Cut large slide mount apart at the seam. Age edges of front cover and slide mount with Warm Violet inkpad. • Stamp "Girl Stuff" using large letter stamps and Wisteria ink on Pink cardstock. Age stamped cardstock with Warm Violet. Tape stamped cardstock to back of mount. Attach mount to cover with foam squares. Flatten bottle caps and attach to corners of mount with E6000. Apply Citrus stickers.

The title, "Katie's Third Grade Photos" has been stamped on a tag and placed in the flap pocket.

Pages 1 & 2 – Looking Good: Cut Pink A-Z Word Blocks 2⅜" x 4½" and glue to flap on left side.
• Cut a horizontal slit in flap 1¾" up from bottom to make the pocket for the disk. • Glue lower edge of flap to bag to create a pocket for the tag. • On right side, cut a curve in the top layer of the bag to allow contents to show. • Age tag and all edges of bag, flap and slit with Wisteria inkpad. Stamp text on tag and tie with ribbon. Tuck into pocket behind flap.
• Drill hole in small metal disk. Cut circle from Lavender cardstock and age with Wisteria. Glue to small metal disk. Flatten Silver bottle cap and glue to disk with E6000. Apply sticker. Tuck into slit pocket. • Mat photo with Lavender cardstock. Age edges with Wisteria. Attach to right side of album with foam tape.
• Cut tag shape from large paint sample card. Punch hole in right edge and tie with ribbon. Decorate with word stickers. Tuck into bag.
Pages 3 & 4 – Here Comes Trouble: Cut Pink A-Z paper 4¼" x 8" and glue across both sides of album.
• Age edges of bag with Peony inkpad. Mat photo with Fuchsia cardstock and attach to left side with foam tape. Age word stickers with Peony and attach to photo with foam squares. • Wrap right side with Magenta ribbon, tucking ends into folds of bag. • Punch a daisy from Fuchsia cardstock and age with Peony ink. Punch hole in daisy and thread with ribbon, knotting and trimming as desired. Glue to right side of album. • Flatten Pink bottle cap and glue to center of daisy with E6000. Apply sticker.
Finish Assembly: Thread ribbon through holes and tie in a knot.

Making a Paper Bag Album

1. Stack bags, alternating placement of openings.

2. Fold bags in half.

3. Punch holes along fold.

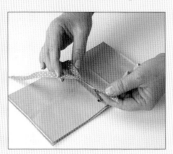

4. Thread ribbon through holes and tie in knots.

What do we love about Katie? Choose word stickers that best tell the story. If you have more to say, cut cardstock to fit the side pocket and write a note.

Pages 5 & 6 – Katie: Cut 5 strips of Pink A-Z paper ⅞" x 2⅝". Age strips and bags with Wisteria ink. Cut five 3" pieces of ribbon. Fold and staple strips and ribbons to flap on left side. Trim ribbons as desired. • Age word stickers with Wisteria ink and attach to strips with foam squares. • Mat photo with Purple cardstock.
• Cut two 3" pieces of ribbon and staple to photo. Attach photo to right side of album with foam tape. Trim ribbons as desired. Write name with metal letters.

Remember the magic you shared and fly back to those special moments with friends every time you look at this fun page.

Pages 7 & 8 – Fly: Attach tulle to both sides of album, tucking under flap and anchoring with brads. Age edges of bag and tulle with Wisteria ink. • Cut around outline of photo and attach to left side of album with foam tape and squares. • Attach tag letters to page with foam squares. Thread Silver floss around brad, through holes in tags, and around second brad, leaving long tails. Trim as desired.
• Cut photo in a circle and glue to 3" metal disk. Drop star sequins into center of disk. Glue button top to disk with E6000. Let dry, without moving sequins. • When dry, fill valley between edge of button and disk with Iris glitter glue. Adhere disk to flap of bag with E6000. • Stamp text with small letter stamps and Wisteria ink.

I understand, Dear. The day's been grand, Dear. But now it's time to sleep. Remember to capture your child catching some "z's" on film so you have photos for occasions such as this.

Pages 9 & 10 – Sleeping: Age edges of bags with Wisteria inkpad. • Mat photo with Pink cardstock. Glue to right side of album. • Trim paint sample cards to desired size. Decorate with word stickers. Attach to pages with White wire clips.

Shadowbox Frames

Shadowbox frames allow you to add memorabilia to a scrapbook layout. The pearls, glove, wand and tiara are too nice to leave out, but are entirely too large to put in a scrapbook album.

Remember how much fun we had that day at the beach? You will when you make this dimensional shadowbox to hang on the wall or decorate a desk.

Princess Wanna Be

MATERIALS: Blue A-Z paper • Stickers: Pink Tag ABCs, Girl Sayings • 4 Pink bottle caps • 12" x 12" shadowbox frame • Cardstock (Pink, White) • Tracing paper • 12" x 12" chipboard • Photos • Plastic tiara • Wand • Pink beads • Sheer Pink glove • Fuchsia silk ⅛" ribbon • Weldbond glue • E6000 adhesive • Foam squares • Glue stick

INSTRUCTIONS:
Glue Blue A-Z paper to chipboard. • Cut hand shape from White cardstock and slip into Pink glove. Mount to bottom of page with foam squares.
• Mat 1 photo with Pink cardstock. • Cut around outline of figure in second photo. Position photos and attach with foam squares. • Adhere wand and tiara in place with E6000. • Print WANNA on tracing paper. Tear edges and glue to page.
• Use tags to spell out PRINCESS, attaching to page with foam squares. Thread ribbon through holes in tags, tie in knots and trim as desired. • Flatten bottle caps, trim with stickers and glue to page.
• Drape beads around glove and under text. Glue in place with Weldbond and let dry completely.
• Insert in shadowbox frame.

Beach Baby

MATERIALS:

Seaside Water paper • Art Words sticker • Brass bottle cap • 6" shadowbox frame • 6" square chipboard • Photo • 2 tiny glass bottles • Sand • Raffia • Seashells • Plastic netting • Tracing paper • Letter stamps • Blue dye inkpad • E6000 adhesive • Foam squares • Tape • Glue stick

INSTRUCTIONS:

Mount Seaside Water paper to chipboard, positioning paper as desired. Trim around edges.
• Cut around figure in photo. Mount to paper with foam squares. • Cut a small piece of net. Drape across bottom of paper. Wrap edges around to back side of chipboard and tape in place. • Tie 3 pieces of raffia in a knot and glue to corner of paper over net.
• Stamp word on tracing paper with letter stamps and dye ink. Let dry. Glue to paper. • Flatten bottle cap and decorate with sticker. Attach to paper with foam square.
• Fill bottles with sand. Seal and tie with raffia. Glue bottles to frame edge with E6000. • Glue shells to frame edge. Let dry.
• Insert photo background into shadowbox.

Dimensions

Too cute! Make this sweet dimensional shadowbox as a gift for Grandma or hang it in the nursery.

Baby Boy

MATERIALS: Mosaic Blue paper • 6 White bottle caps • Blue ABCs stickers • 3 Blue Clothespins • 8" x 10" shadowbox frame • Foam core • Navy cardstock • Baby hat and sock • Square acrylic bead box • Lock of hair • Silk ribbon • Straight pins • E6000 adhesive • Foam squares • Glue stick

INSTRUCTIONS:

Cut a piece of foam core 8" x 10". • Cover with Mosaic Blue paper. • Mat photo with Navy cardstock. • Position hat, photo and sock on page. Attach hat and sock to page with straight pins through fabric into foam core. • Adhere photo with foam dots.
• Attach bottle caps to page with E6000. Decorate with stickers.
• Attach acrylic bead box to page with E6000. Fill with lock of baby's hair tied with silk ribbon. • Clip clothespins to hat. • When all glue is dry, insert foam core into shadowbox.

Pocket Calendars

Life is brighter when you surround yourself with ordinary items decorated with your favorite photos.

Baby Pocket Calendar
MATERIALS: Baby Bubbles Blue paper • Blue Words stickers • Pocket calendar cover • Blue cardstock • Photo • Glue stick
INSTRUCTIONS: Remove calendar from plastic cover. • Cover with Baby Bubbles Blue paper. Trim edges. • Mat photo with Blue cardstock. Glue to cover. • Decorate with stickers. • When dry, insert into plastic cover.

Girl Pocket Calendar
MATERIALS: Papers: Pink A-Z, Pink A-Z Word Blocks • Princess stickers • Pocket calendar • Photo • Glue stick
INSTRUCTIONS: Remove calendar from plastic cover. Cover with Pink A-Z paper. Cut a strip of Pink A-Z Word Blocks and glue to cover. Trim edges. • Cut around outline of figure in photo, glue to cover. • Decorate with stickers. When dry, insert into cover.

Boy Pocket Calendar
MATERIALS: Lime A-Z Word Blocks paper • Real Boy stickers • Pocket calendar • Blue cardstock • Photo • Ribbon • Glue stick
INSTRUCTIONS: Remove calendar from plastic cover. Cover with Lime A-Z Word Blocks paper. Trim edges. • Wrap cover with ribbon, overlapping just left of center and gluing in place. Cover overlap with sticker. • Mat photo with Blue cardstock and glue to cover, tucking under ribbon. • When dry, insert into plastic cover.

Decorating a Calendar Cover

1. Remove calendar from plastic cover.

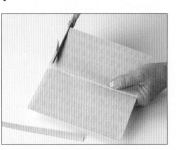

2. Cover outside with paper.

3. Trim edges.

4. Decorate with photos, papers and stickers.

5. Reinsert into cover.

Baby's Journa

MATERIALS: Paper Baby Books, 1 B Milestones • 2 Victor printed mounts • Ma mini file folders: 1 sma large • Pink clothespin Pink bottle caps Stickers: Girls Sayi Pink Words • Vari small photos • Pink lets • Blue ¼" organza bon • Ecru lace • Pink berry paper • *Color* pigment inks (Colo Blue, Pink) • Black point marker • Pink ored pencil • Eyelet • Scissors • Craft knif Small tag punch • H gun • Foam squares, strips

INSTRUCTIONS:
Cut Baby Books paper 3 horizontal strips. Create a lift on the p that has "To The Baby" and Pink ribbon each corner by cuttin slit around the edges flowers and bows. • out inside of frame "Baby Book". Glue ph to back side of paper mat. • Fold each im strip in half and open Fold the right and edges to meet at the ter fold and glue do Fold in half. Make sure do not glue down the area on the one b cover image. • Rep same steps with other strips of paper. Nest three folded pieces and together with Blue or za ribbon.
Decorate inside of boo
Page 1: Tear a co portion of B Milestones paper. Ap Pink and Blue ink to edge. Apply glue to ed only and adhere to pag to create pocket. E page with Pink and ink. Edge smallest min folder with Blue ink place in pocket. Ap

Baby's Mini-Journal

by Michele Charles

Here's a baby brag book with an elegant flair. It contains baby photos with embellishments.

word stickers. Flatten bottle cap, apply sticker and attach to page with foam square.

Page 2: Edge with Blue ink.

Page 3: Edge page with Pink ink. Punch 3 small tags from photos. Set Pink eyelets on tags. Tie Blue organza ribbon to each tag. Attach each tag to page with a foam square. Tie all 3 ribbons together and clip with Pink clothespin. Glue clothespin to page.

Page 4: Edge page with Pink ink. Edge largest mini file folder with Pink ink. Apply heart and word sticker to folder. Wrap Blue organza ribbon around file folder and tie a bow. Glue folder to page.

Page 5: Edge page with Pink ink. Glue photo to page. Adhere lace around photo.

Page 6: Edge with Pink ink. Edge small Pink slide mount and tag with Blue ink. Heat set ink. Glue photo to back of slide mount. Apply glue to back of slide mount. Place slide mount under created lifts of flowers and ribbons in each corner. Tie Blue organza ribbon to tag. Attach tag to page with foam square. Attach word stickers to slide mount and tag.

Page 7: Edge page with Pink ink. Cut around image of little girl. Cut out bow and ribbon from matching book cover on Baby Books paper. Glue bow to top of little girl image. Attach to page with foam squares.

Page 8: Edge small slide mount with Blue ink and heat set. Glue photo to back of mount and glue to page. Attach word sticker to mount. Flatten Pink bottle cap, apply sticker and attach to page with foam square.

Page 9: Edge with Pink ink. Write name on page with Pink colored pencil, accent drop shadow with Black fine tip marker. Tear edges of mulberry paper. Glue photo to mulberry photo and then glue to page.

Page 10: Edge with Blue ink. Tie a Blue organza ribbon bow and glue to page.

Pages 1 and 2

Pages 3 and 4

Pages 5 and 6

Pages 7 and 8

Pages 9 and 10

Back of Album

MATERIALS:
Papers: Blue A-Z Word Blocks, Blue A-Z, Lime A-Z, Boy Blue • Bottle caps: 1 Aqua, 5 Lime, 6 Silver, 4 Navy • Stickers: Blue ABCs, Boy Sayings, Blue Tag ABCs, Kids Words, Blue Words, Real Boy • 2 Blue metal clips • Blue wire clip • Slide Mounts: 1 large Color Game, 4 small White • Brown paper bags (3 lunch size, 1 small 2⅝" wide) • Cardstock (Burgundy, Ivory, Navy, Teal) • Photos • Assorted striped ribbons • White eyelets • 5 White eyelets • Assorted brads • Metal-rimmed tags • *Ranger* Walnut Distress ink • Hole punch • Clamps • Stapler • Eyelet tools • Foam squares • Glue stick

INSTRUCTIONS:
To Make the Album:
Layer 3 bags on top of each other, alternating open side of bags. Fold bags in half. Clamp folded bags to hold in place. Glue 1" strip of Burgundy cardstock to folded edge of bag. Punch holes through cardstock strip 1¼" apart. Set White eyelets in holes. Tie ribbons through eyelets. Randomly age edges of all bags with Distress ink.
• Decorate pages as desired.

**Pattern for
Paper Pocket**

cut 2

How to Make a Paper Pocket

1. Trace pattern on back side of paper.

2. Cut out pieces.

3. Fold front of pocket along 3 sides.

4. Age pieces with chalk inkpad.

5. Glue front of pocket to back.

Paper Bag Album

by Robin Carsey

Here's a truly interactive scrapbook. Every page engages the viewer with a pull-out tab revealing interesting photos and embellishments.

How to Cover a Slide Mount

1. Glue mount to wrong side of paper.

2. Trim around outer edge of mount.

3. Cut an 'X' in center of mount.

4. Fold tabs of paper back, glue.

5. Trim away excess paper.

Clipboard & Journal

Use a clipboard as a frame. Bring out photos and display them in an appealing way.

MATERIALS:
7 Lime bottle caps • 3" metal disk • Stickers: Citrus Brights, Blue Words • Papers: Blue A-Z Word Blocks, Blue A-Z, Lime A-Z Word Blocks • 9" x 12½" Clipboard • Green paint sample card • Assorted ribbons • Photo • Green notepad • Plexiglass • Letter stamps • Blue spray paint • Black pigment ink • Heat gun • Foam squares • Tacky glue • E6000 adhesive • Glue stick

INSTRUCTIONS:
Spray paint clipboard Blue and let dry completely. • Cut rectangle Blue A-Z paper to fit clipboard, rounding corners. Glue to clipboard, tucking under clamp. Cut strip of Lime A-Z Word Blocks and glue to lower section of clipboard, wrapping around edges to back side.
• Glue paint sample card to left side of clipboard, tucking under clamp.
• Position photo on clipboard. Glue in place, or attach with removable double-sided tape. Cover photo with Plexiglass, using clamp to hold in place.
• Position stickers on Plexiglass, overlapping edge of photo. • Stamp letters on bottle caps with Black pigment ink. Set ink with heat tool. Position caps on clipboard, and hold in place with 2 stacked foam squares.
• Cut pieces of ribbon and tuck under edges of caps, holding in place with a dab of Tacky glue. • Glue notepad to clipboard. • Cut circle from Blue A-Z Word Blocks paper and glue to center of metal disk. Glue to clipboard with E6000, tucking pieces of ribbon under disk.
• Flatten 2 Lime bottle caps, and attach to disk and clipboard clamp using foam squares. Decorate flattened caps with stickers.

Dear Diary, Mom made this neat book for me for my birthday. I really love it. Now I have a place to keep all my secrets.

MATERIALS:
3 Silver bottle caps • Pink wire clip • 2⅜" metal disk • Princess stickers • Papers: Pink A-Z Word Blocks, Pink A-Z • 7½" x 9½" composition book • Lavender cardstock • 5" x 7" photo • Lavender sheer ribbon • Purple duct tape • Purple paint sample card • *ColorBox* Fluid Chalk inkpads (Wisteria, Peony) • Foam squares • Glue stick

INSTRUCTIONS:
Cover front and back of book with Pink A-Z paper. • Cut photo in semi-circle, mount to Lavender cardstock and trim to desired width. Age edges of cardstock with Wisteria inkpad. Glue to center front of book.
• Cut 2 Pink A-Z Word Blocks 4" x 7½" and glue to lower section of front and back of book, overlapping photo in front. • Trim around outer edges of book. • Cut a strip of Purple duct tape slightly longer than spine of book. Apply tape to spine, centering. Trim to size. • Attach paint sample card to book with wire clip, gluing in place if desired. • Tie sheer ribbon around front cover of book, tying in knot and trimming tails as desired.
• Cut circle of Pink A-Z paper to fit inside the metal disk. Age with Peony inkpad. Glue to center of metal disk. • Flatten bottle caps and adhere to book with foam squares. Apply stickers to caps.

1. Glue paper to cover. Line up against binding.

2. Trim paper to book edges.

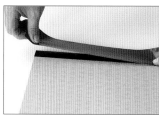

3. Apply new binding. Overlap paper slightly.

4. Trim binding at top and bottom of spine.

I like my work to look unique so I choose to enhance purchased papers. Here are some ideas for individualizing your papers.

Distressing Papers

Making Papers Your Own

1. Tear paper and apply chalks or inks to torn edges.
2. Crumple paper. Flatten slightly and apply chalk inks lightly to surface. When dry, iron paper to flatten completely.
3. Apply acrylic paints to edges of paper with dry bristle brush, dragging color to create streaks.
4. Glue paper to cardstock backing and sand with medium weight sandpaper or sanding block.
5. Apply chalk inks to edges to create an aged look. Drag color across paper to create uneven streaks and blotches.

6. Drag alcohol ink pads across paper. Spritz with water using a spray bottle. Iron flat.
7. Stamp paper with chunky stamps and inks or acrylics.
8. Apply White gesso or acrylic paint to edges of paper with dry bristle brush, dragging paint across paper to create streaks.
9. Paint paper with strong coffee. While still damp, sprinkle instant coffee crystals on paper.
10. Sand paper with sanding block. Drag chalk ink pad over sanded areas.
11. Spray through Magic Mesh with spray paint.
12. Drag colored glazes across paper with bristle brush.

Easy-to-Make Holiday Journal

Keep track of your gift and card lists, or who has been naughty and nice in this festive holiday journal.

MATERIALS:
Papers: Green Holly, Holidays Bottle Caps • 3" metal disk • Holidays 2 transparency • Stickers: Holiday Sayings, Christmas • Vintage Books slide mount • Composition book • Dark Green cardstock • Index tabs • Photo • Red ribbon • Gesso • Foam dots • Tape • Glue stick

INSTRUCTIONS:
Cut two 2¼" strips of Green Holly paper and glue to front and back outer edge of the journal cover.
• Cut a ½" strip of Dark Green cardstock and glue over edge of Green Holly. Cut a 10½" piece of Holidays paper and glue to journal, wrapping around from front to back.
• Paint metal disk with gesso. While wet, cut circle from transparency and place in center of lid. Let dry.
• Trim photo to size and tape to back of large mount. Apply foam dots to back of metal disk, slide mount and December 25th sticker. Position on journal as desired. Tie bow from ribbon and glue to top of lid.
• Apply index tabs to pages. Add a sticker to each tab.

How to Cover a 4-Pack Holder

1. Fold paper in half, and clip halfway up center.

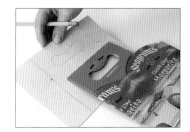

2. Place folded paper over 4-pack holder top, and trace sides and opening.

3. Trim paper on sides, creating tabs, and cut out opening.

4. Glue in place, folding tabs inward.

5. Wrap patterned paper around bottom section and glue in place.

Sara 4-Pack

MATERIALS:
Container: Baby Stripes paper • Pink bottle cap • Stickers: Girl Sayings, Pink Tag ABCs • 4-pack holder • Pink cardstock • Assorted Pink ribbons • Stapler • Foam tape • Glue stick
Filling: Pink baby socks • Pink teddy bear • Pink baby bottle • Pink jelly beans • Pink baby washcloths

INSTRUCTIONS:
Cover base of 4-pack with Baby Stripes paper and handle with Pink cardstock.
• Cut short pieces of ribbons and staple to side of holder. Tie soft bow around handle with ribbon.
• Flatten bottle cap and adhere to handle with foam tape. Attach sticker to cap. Thread sheer ribbon through holes in tag stickers and apply to holder with foam tape. • Fill baby bottle with Pink jelly beans. • If items sink too low in holder, fill bottom with tissue paper.

Baby Girl Can

MATERIALS
Baby Bubbles Pink paper • Pink clothespins • Pink satin ribbon • White tulle • Small paint can • Paint can key • E6000 adhesive • Glue stick

INSTRUCTIONS:
Cut Baby Bubbles paper the height of paint can. Adhere to can using glue stick. • Tear a small piece of paper and glue to cover gap. Cut circle of paper to fit in lid of the can and adhere with glue stick. • Fill can and tap lid in place with a mallet. • Tie White tulle around can, trimming ends to desired length. • Tie a multi loop bow with long tails from satin. Tie in place around tulle with piece of satin ribbon.
• Tie paint can key to one long tail.
• Clip clothespins to ribbon.

Baby Boy Can

MATERIALS
Baby Bubbles Blue paper • Silver bottle cap • 2⅜" metal disk • Boy Sayings sticker • Small paint can • Paint can key • Blue Gingham ribbon • E6000 • Glue stick

Baby Boy Can - INSTRUCTIONS:
Cut Baby Bubbles paper the height of the paint can. Adhere to can with glue stick. • Tear a small piece of paper and glue to cover gap. • Wrap top edge of can with ribbon, gluing in place. • Tie a multi-loop bow with long tails and glue over join in ribbon. • Flatten bottle cap and decorate with sticker. Glue over center of bow.
• Tie paint key to one tail of ribbon. Clip remaining tails to desired length. • Cut circle of paper to fit in lid of can and adhere with glue stick. • Cut photo to fit in center of metal disk and adhere with glue stick. Adhere to lid with E6000.

Special Baby Gifts

Presentation is the key to successful gift giving. Welcome that extra special bundle of joy with a great baby gift in these unique packages.

Dangles Photo

by Carrie Avery

Hang this vacation photo on your computer and take a trip back to someplace wonderful every day. The key to charming dangles is in your choice of images.

MATERIALS:
Papers: TeaDye Script, da Vinci Brocade, Vintage Bottle Caps • 3 Gold bottle caps • Silver metal clip • Coffee Words sticker) • 5½" x 8" chipboard • 3½" x 5" photo • Plexiglass • Lace • Assorted ribbon • 10" Silver chain • Charms (Key, Pen nib) • 11 Silver eyelets • Five 2" Silver eye pins • Assorted beads • Eyelet tools • Round-nose pliers • Wire cutters • Hole punch (1" circle, ⅛", ¹⁄₁₆") • Glue stick

INSTRUCTIONS:
Board: Cover chipboard with Brocade and Script papers, wrapping to the back. • Adhere ribbon over the intersection of the papers. Adhere lace above the ribbon. Set eyelets in the 4 corners and across the bottom of the chipboard.
• Cover postcard with plexiglass and position it in the center of the chipboard. Mark the position for 4 eyelets. Set eyelets. Reposition the postcard and plexiglass, wrapping ribbon through the eyelets to hold it in place. Add sticker and Silver clip to the plexiglass.
Dangles: Punch a ¹⁄₁₆" hole in the bottle caps. Cut 1" circles from Vintage paper. Adhere circles inside caps. • Attach bottle caps or charms to the end of each eye pin. String on beads. Pass eye pin through the eyelet and wrap the end around itself. Trim as needed.

Wedding Paint Can

MATERIALS:
Papers: Romance Celebration, 2 sheets of Rom
License • Vintage printed Slide Mounts • Letter Sq
Cutable Strip • Photos • Gallon paint can • Paint
opener • Assorted ribbons (White, Cream, Gold) •
letters • Manila tags • *ColorBox* Yellow Ochre •
Chalk inkpad • Tin snips • Foam squares • Glue sti

INSTRUCTIONS:
Age the top edge of 2 sheets of Romance License
with chalk inkpad. Cover upper section of paint can
aged paper, lining up edges with sides of can and
ming around handles.
• Cut Romance Celebration in half to create 2 piec
high. Tear top edges of papers so they are high o

Wedding 4-Pack

MATERIALS:
Container: Romance Celebration paper • Cardboa
pack • Cardstock (Ivory, White) • Pearls • White tu
Ivory sheer ribbon • String • Small White tags • Si
Rub-ons words • Wire • Hole punch • Glue stick
Filling: 2 champagne glasses • Split of champagne •
candle • Gold shred

INSTRUCTIONS:
Cover base of 4-pack with \Romance Celebration p
and handle with Ivory cardstock. (See page 30.) •

r edges and lower in center. Age edges with
k inkpad. Glue to bottom of paint can, overlap-
Romance License paper. • Print photos in Sepia
. Trim one photo and tape to back side of mount.
mount with chalk inkpad. Attach to front of can
foam squares. Add names to mount using metal
rs. • Cut short pieces of ribbon and tie to han-
Cut longer pieces and tie to bottoms of handle as
amers. • Cut photo in shape of tag, age and
ch to handle. • Decorate small tag with Cutables
ls. Age with chalk inkpad and attach to handle.
t slit in paint can lid with tin snips. Cut a circle
omance Celebration paper to fit inside rim. Age
e with chalk inkpad and glue to lid, slitting paper
tucking inside opening.
t letters from Cutables strip and glue to lid.

photo on White cardstock and cut into tag shape,
punching hole at top. • Apply rub-ons to printed
tag, small White tags and handle of holder. • Tie
tulle and sheer ribbon around holder, making a soft
bow. • Punch a small hole in corner of holder, and
slide wire through hole and over center of bow.
Thread pearls onto wire, wrap around corner of
holder and twist to tighten in place. • Thread tags
onto string, and tie to corner of holder under bow.
• Fill champagne glasses with gold shred. Place
glasses, champagne and candle in holder.

Wedding & Anniversary Gifts

Now and forever, these gifts have everything you need for a can-
dlelit celebration. Bedecked in white and gold, this 4-pack and
can make pleasing presents. Make them really special with beau-
tiful decorations, for a perfect centerpiece on the table!

Treasure Book

by Michele Charles

Create themed shadowbox art with canvas and coordinated papers.

MATERIALS:
3 Circus 9" x 9" cardstock • Cutable Doo-dads: Letter Squares, Toy Blocks, Dark Words, Light Words • Salsa printed mount • Black Wire Clip • Red bottle cap • Two 6" x 6" canvases • Black and White photo printed on White glossy cardstock • Small photos (Color, Black and White) • Red cardstock • Small glass bottle • 6 buttons • Waxed Linen • *Ranger* (Distress Inks: Vintage Photo, Black Soot, Peeled Paint, Fired Brick, Antique Linen; Glossy Accents; Bottle of Green Adirondack acrylic paint) • Stamps (*River City Rubber Works* unmounted letter stamps; *Magenta* Corner Stamp; *Paper Artsy* text stamp) • *ColorBox* Pink pigment ink • 6 nails • Scissors • Craft knife • Paper towels • 1" round punch • Scrapper's sanding Block • *Therm O Web* Adhesive foam squares • E6000 adhesive • *Crafter's Pick* The Ultimate! glue